DEER!

A MY INCREDIBLE WORLD PICTURE BOOK

MY INCREDIBLE WORLD

www.myincredibleworld.com

Deer are native to every continent in the world, except for Australia and Antarctica.

They live in many different habitats, including wetlands, forests, grasslands and mountains.

The scientific name for the deer family is **Cervidae**, which also includes elk, moose and caribou.

There are at least 43 different species of deer (also called **cervids**).

All deer have 2 large and
2 small hooves on each foot!

Deer have elongated, horizontal pupils that let them keep a panoramic lookout for predators!

They are **crepuscular**, meaning they are most active around dusk and dawn.

Deer are **herbivores** because they only like to eat plants.

They are very social animals, and usually live in groups called **herds**.

A female deer is called a **doe**.

A male deer is called a **buck**.

Female deer usually have 1 to 3 babies (called **fawns**) each year!

Fawns are typically born between April and June.

They weigh only 4 to 8 pounds (2 to 4 kg) at birth (similar to a human baby)!

Newborn fawns can stand at around 10 minutes old and can walk at only 7 hours old!

For most species of deer, only males have **antlers** (females do not).

Antlers are made of bone,
and are shed (and regrown)
every year!

New antlers are covered
with velvety fur that
eventually wears away.

Deer can run up to 35 miles per hour (56 kph) — about as fast as a car!

Deer are excellent swimmers, and sometimes stay in water to avoid predators!

They have an amazing sense of smell and can detect some odors up to a half mile away!

Deer are incredible!

Made in United States
North Haven, CT
17 December 2023

On the first day of Christma … gave to me:

It's me.
I'm the problem.
It's me.

On the second day of Christmas, Taylor gave to me:

Red: Taylor's Version

And it's me. I'm the problem. It's me.

On the third day of Christmas, Taylor gave to me:
A Chiefs Tight End
87

Red: Taylor‘s version.

And it’s me. I’m the problem. It’s me.

On the fourth day of Christmas,
Taylor gave to me:
Beaded friendship bracelets

A Chiefs Tight End.
Red: Taylor‘s version.
And it’s me. I’m the problem. It’s me.

On the fifth day of Christmas, Taylor gave to me:

WHY CAN'T WE HAVE NICE THINGS?!

Beaded friendship bracelets.
A Chiefs Tight End.
Red: Taylor‘s version.
And it’s me. I’m the problem. It’s me.

On the sixth day of Christmas, Taylor gave to me:
The scarf kept in his dresser

WHY CAN'T WE HAVE NICE THINGS?!

Beaded friendship bracelets.
A Chiefs Tight End.
Red: Taylor's version.
And it's me. I'm the problem. It's me.

On the seventh day of Christmas,
Taylor gave to me:
I'm on the bleachers

The scarf kept in his dresser.

WHY CAN'T WE HAVE NICE THINGS?!

Beaded friendship bracelets.
A Chiefs Tight End.
Red: Taylor's version.
And it's me. I'm the problem. It's me.

On the eighth day of Christmas, Taylor gave to me:
Romeo kneeling

I‘m on the bleachers.
The scarf kept in his dresser.

WHY CAN‘T WE HAVE NICE THINGS?!

Beaded friendship bracelets.
A Chiefs Tight End.
Red: Taylor‘s version.
And it’s me. I’m the problem. It’s me.

On the ninth day of Christmas,
Taylor gave to me:
Me & Karma vibe-ing

Romeo kneeling.
I'm on the bleachers.
The scarf kept in his dresser.

WHY CAN'T WE HAVE NICE THINGS?!

Beaded friendship bracelets.
A Chiefs Tight End.
Red: Taylor's version.
And it's me. I'm the problem. It's me.

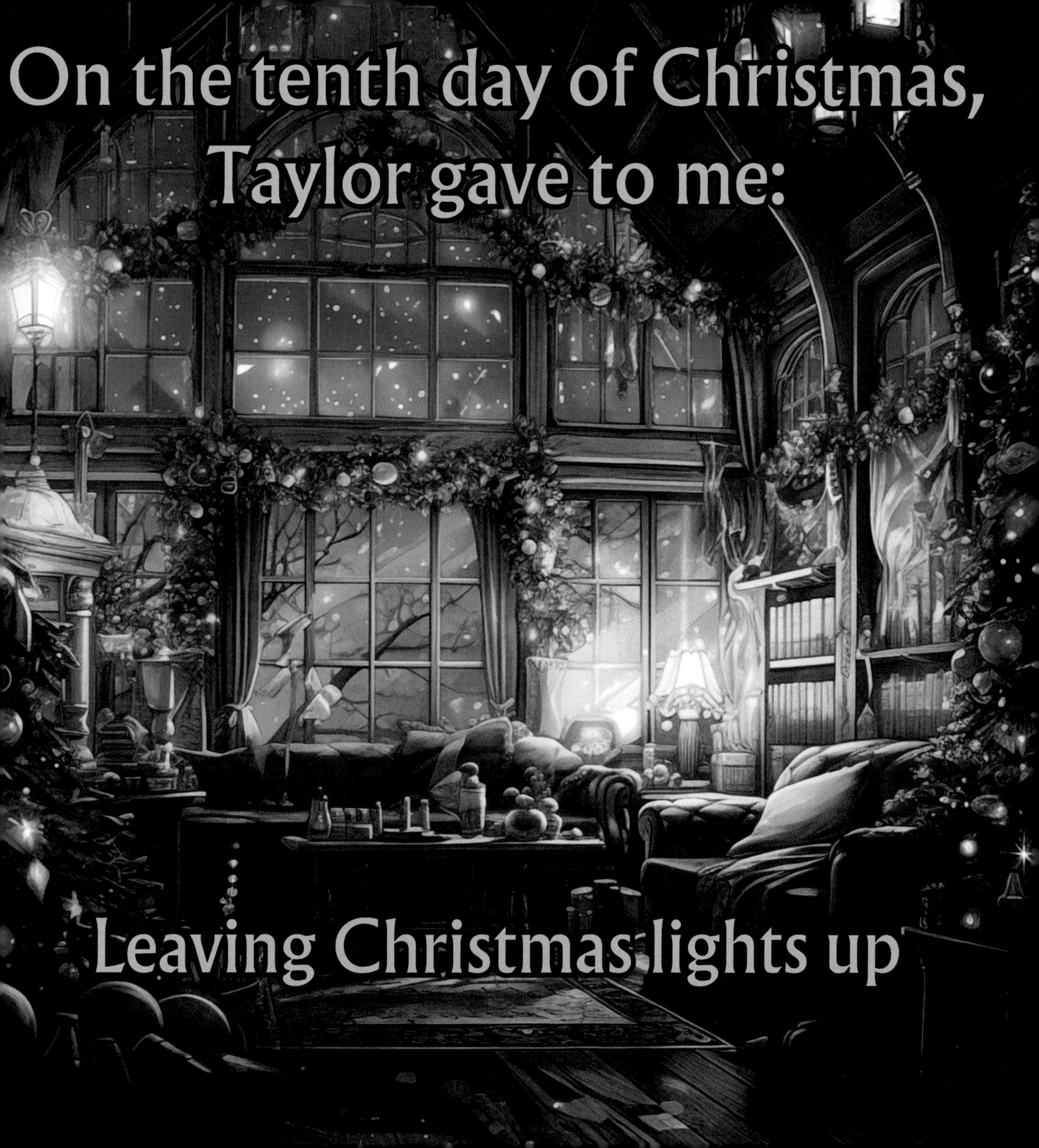
On the tenth day of Christmas,
Taylor gave to me:
Leaving Christmas lights up

Me & Karma vibe-ing.
Romeo kneeling.
I'm on the bleachers.
The scarf kept in his dresser.

WHY CAN'T WE HAVE NICE THINGS?!

Beaded friendship bracelets.
A Chiefs Tight End.
Red: Taylor's version.
And it's me. I'm the problem. It's me.

On the eleventh day of Christmas, Taylor gave to me:

Glitter after the party

Leaving Christmas lights up.
Me & Karma vibe-ing.
Romeo kneeling.
I‘m on the bleachers.
The scarf kept in his dresser.

WHY CAN‘T WE HAVE NICE THINGS?!

Beaded friendship bracelets.
A Chiefs Tight End.
Red: Taylor‘s version.
And it’s me. I’m the problem. It’s me.

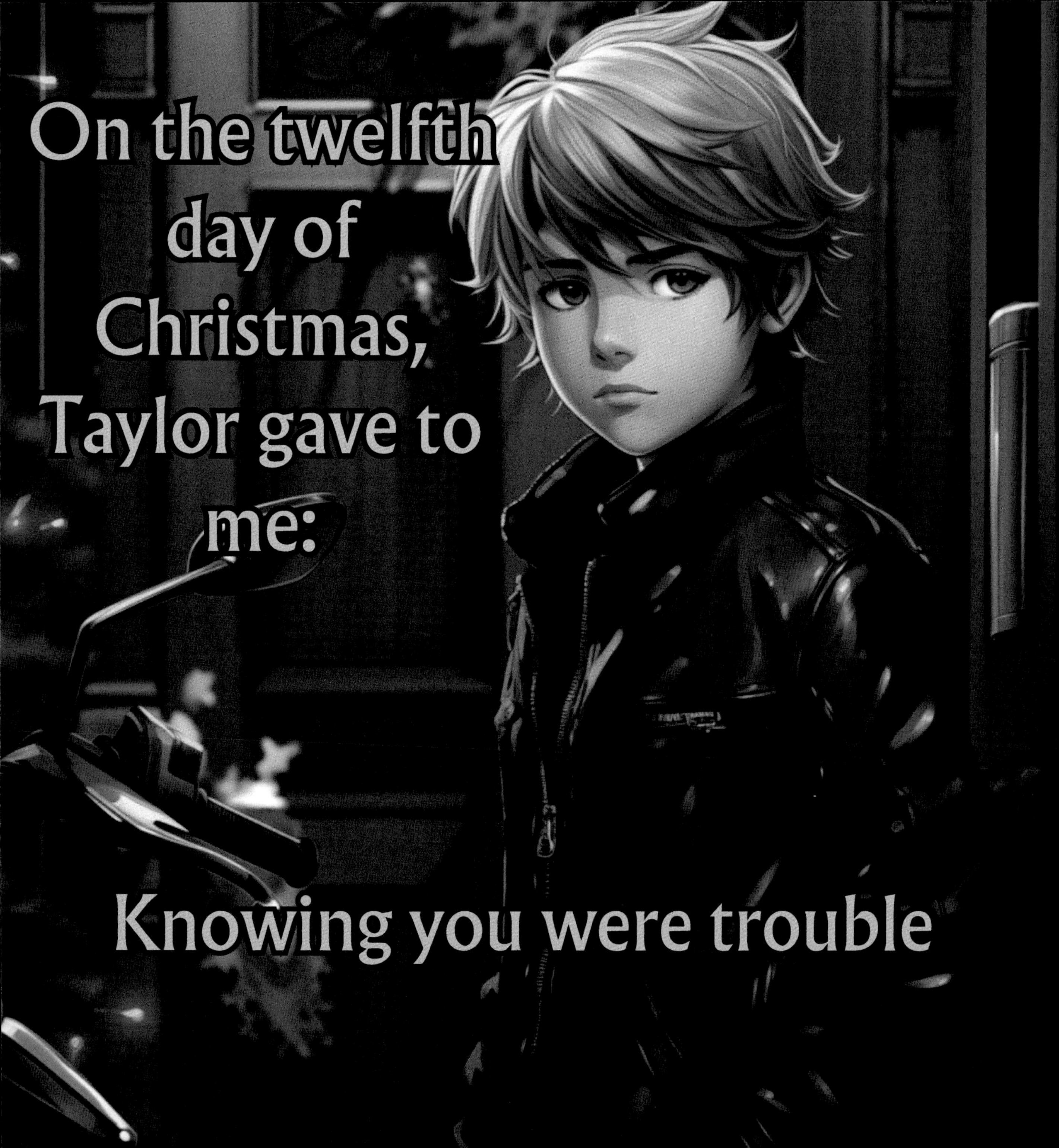
On the twelfth
day of
Christmas,
Taylor gave to
me:
Knowing you were trouble

Glitter after the party.
Leaving Christmas lights up.
Me & Karma vibe-ing.
Romeo kneeling.
I‘m on the bleachers.
The scarf kept in his dresser.

WHY CAN‘T WE HAVE NICE THINGS?!

Beaded friendship bracelets.
A Chiefs Tight End.
Red: Taylor‘s version.
And it’s me. I’m the problem. It’s me.

Knowing you were trouble.
Glitter after the party.
Leaving Christmas lights up.
Me & Karma vibe-ing.
Romeo kneeling.
I'm on the bleachers.
The scarf kept in his dresser.
WHY CAN'T WE HAVE NICE THINGS?!
Beaded friendship bracelets.
A Chiefs Tight End.
Red: Taylor's version.
And it's me. I'm the problem. It's me.

Made in United States
Orlando, FL
06 December 2024